MW00437662

Hiding behind the Mask

Hiding
behind the Mask

In the Corporate Closet *with* Cancer

KAY HOLLEMAN

BROWN BOOKS PUBLISHING GROUP
DALLAS, TEXAS

Hiding behind the Mask
In the Corporate Closet with Cancer

© 2006 Kay Holleman
Written by Kay Holleman.
www.hidingbehindthemask.com

Manufactured in the United States.

For information, please contact:
Brown Books Publishing Group
16200 North Dallas Parkway, Suite 170
Dallas, Texas 75248
www.brownbooks.com
972-381-0009
A New Era in Publishing™

ISBN: 1-933285-30-3
LCCN 2005909582
1 2 3 4 5 6 7 8 9 10

First Printing, 2006

For Kristi McIntyre, MD, and
G. Thomas Shires, III, MD

God was watching when our paths crossed
You have kept me safe
Today a new sun rises for me
I am forever grateful

Contents

ACKNOWLEDGMENTS

I would like to humbly acknowledge my parents, Sidney and Katherine, whose unconditional love and keen wisdom taught me that anything is possible if you only believe in yourself. I wish to express my deep love for my brother Sid, his wife Janice, my nephew Steve, and my nieces Stacy and Shelly, all of whom have been my anchors. I would like to extend my profound gratitude to Milli A. Brown, publisher and believer, and her "team" at Brown Books Publishing Group— Kathryn Grant, Cindy Birne, Erica Jennings, Deanne Dice, and Brian McKay. Also, I wish to express my deep appreciation for Rhonda

Porterfield, MD, who guided me every step of the way. I would like to honor my dear friend, Toni Ratliff, a woman who gives new meaning to the word survivor. And finally, I wish to acknowledge cancer survivors . . . those gone before, those present, and those yet to come.

Introduction:

Burning Still Higher

Our inward power, when it obeys nature,
reacts to events by accommodating itself to
what it faces—to what is possible. It needs
no specific material. It pursues its own aims
as circumstances allow; it turns obstacles into
fuel. As a fire overwhelms what would have
quenched a lamp. What's thrown on top of the
conflagration is absorbed, consumed by it—
and makes it burn still higher.

~Marcus Aurelius

Cancer gave me an edge. For twenty years, I dealt with it in secret, not merely meeting my responsibilities as a bank executive, but exceeding them. I have been treated for breast cancer three times since the age of thirty-nine, and yet I've never been sick a day in my life. My cancer and my career intertwined, each transforming the other into something distinctive and unconventional. Neither would have run the same course without the other.

When I use the term "my cancer," I mean it genuinely, in the sense that it is mine. It is not an alien entity, not a thing that is anti-Kay, but an authentic part of Kay. My cancer made me more than I was before. My sickness did not transform me into a sick person—rather, I transformed it into my coach, my motivator, my mentor. Cancer urged me onward. It trained me to be clever and inventive and resourceful. It granted me wisdom and insight. Indeed, I used cancer to enrich my life.

Many factors contributed to my success in dealing with cancer. First is my "angel corps," my cherished friends: Julie Insaustegui, Johnlyn Mitchell, Jackie Porter, Toni Ratliff, and Ginny Walker. These faithful women supported me and cared for me daily, always helping me find humor in the bleakest of times. My brother, Dr. Sid A. Holleman, Jr., was ever at my side to listen and advise. The legacy of my early years—my mother's gracious dignity and my father's pithy wisdom—was of incalculable value. My mother's sister, Rubye T. Ellington, has been more mother than aunt to me over the past thirty years. Her wisdom and love have sustained me, and her fortitude as a woman ahead of her time has amazed me. Any list of dear ones must also include my beloved cat, VP, who was a constant comfort to me. Most of all, my faith, my personal spirituality, served as the foundation for my decisions, my courage, and my very survival.

I don't dismiss my experience with cancer as painless or trivial. Yet neither did I set aside those years as a time of invasion by something dark and sinister. On the contrary, I assimilated cancer into my life. The treatment, the modifications to my behavior, and the concessions to my lifestyle are so much a part of me that I cannot imagine my life otherwise. Having cancer was the best thing that ever happened to me. I'll celebrate anything with anybody, anytime. Right now, I'd like to celebrate with you the richness of my life—a life lived in the corporate closet with cancer.

1:

WHEN JARRED . . .

When jarred, unavoidably, by circumstances, revert at once to yourself, and don't lose the rhythm more than you can help. You'll have a better grasp of the harmony if you keep on going back to it.

~Marcus Aurelius

"You have such a mischievous look in your eyes. Are you always in trouble, or do you just look like it?" I heard that question from the nuns at Our Lady of Victory Academy in Fort Worth, Texas, more than once. Actually, you could see the answer by looking at my knees. They had permanent ruts from having to kneel for penitence in front of the classroom.

One morning, when I was in grade school, they assigned me to help out in the kitchen where an elderly nun was preparing wafers for communion. I hadn't had much breakfast that particular day, and as I watched her pour batter into the waffle-iron cooker, my stomach growled. Although communion crackers tend to lack flavor, they did fill the air with the aroma of fresh-baked pastry. As I helped her transfer them to bowls, I sneaked a handful for myself and stuffed them into my mouth. I tried another handful a moment later, and soon developed a sort of cadence—some for the bowl, some for me, some for the bowl, some for me. The nun didn't understand why she couldn't get ahead with her baking, and she kept repeating, "I just don't know why this is taking so long today." I didn't get in trouble that day—I didn't get caught!

My enthusiasm wasn't limited to mischief. I've always entered into each endeavor wholeheartedly; thus, in spite of my adventuresome spirit, I was a good student. My nonconformist streak may have driven the nuns to distraction, but I worked as hard as I played, and I achieved the office of president of the student council my senior year at Nolan High School. That combination of unconventionality and diligence, living outside the rules but succeeding in the system, has always worked for me.

I follow the path that my own personal philosophy dictates. One of my tenets is that our lives consist only of a moment. Not a series of moments, not days, or years, or decades, but just one single moment. That's all you can live at one time. You can't capture a moment and live it when you're more prepared for it. You can't skip a disagreeable one here and there, or hold onto a spectacular one and live it over and over. Life is what it is. A moment.

I choose to live this moment in happiness. Yes, one chooses to be happy, just as one chooses to be a banker, or a realtor, or a teacher. Although having cancer was not my choice, I chose how I managed it. Not knowing how other people dealt with it, I made up my own rules. I never thought of myself as a trailblazer, but looking back, I see that I was—in more ways than one.

There were very few officer-level women in banking in the early days of my career. I did not originally see myself in the corporate world. Before I was a banker, I was a realtor, and before that, a teacher. I graduated from the University of North Texas with a Bachelor of Science degree. After four years of teaching high school in the Dallas-Fort Worth metroplex, I grew weary of the tenure salary system and the dismal prospects for future financial advancement. I was happy to take my father's offer to join his real estate business, Gulfside Management Company, in Port Aransas, Texas. As vice president of sales, I immediately took to the pitches, the marketing, the deals—all so different from teaching. The work satisfied my desire for incentive-based achievement and sparked my interest in the business world. During that time, I completed a master's degree at the University of North Texas.

I was about twenty-seven years old, enjoying the real estate business, when my mother became ill with cardiomyopathy. She was a relatively young woman at the time, only fifty-eight. Never suspecting that she would serve as a role model for my own illness, I nonetheless learned from her graceful acceptance of a serious disease. She was never angry about it, never questioned why. The one sorrow that elegant lady expressed was that her grandchildren would not remember her.

I stayed with my parents constantly during the three years of my mother's illness. Hindsight shows me that I never made a concrete decision to opt for a career and forego a family of my own. Instead, various circumstances guided me, perhaps beginning with that intense time of caring for my mother and helping my father.

Before my mother eventually succumbed in 1976, she had several close calls with death. Her accounts of some of those experiences have been a comfort to me over the years. Once she recalled feeling herself walking upstairs toward a warm, bright light. She kept looking back down, and then a voice said, "Not now, Katherine." Another time, in the hospital, she felt herself being lifted off the bed toward the ceiling. She looked down, saw the family standing around her bed, and was drawn back. She told me later, "You have nothing to fear of death. I experienced wonderful feelings of peace and joy."

Early on, I had considered medicine as a career, but my mother's unrelenting medical interventions and hospitalizations drained any interest I had in the subject. Despite my plans to the contrary, though, the field of medicine has, in an unexpected way, filled a large part of my life.

In the fall of 1974, two years before my mother's death, I took a job with a well-respected financial institution, the largest bank in the region at that time, in Dallas, Texas. Judge Sarah T. Hughes, a stockholder in the company, had brought attention to the fact that there were no female executive officers at this particular bank. Fortunately for me, they decided to search for women with master's degrees who they thought stood a chance of being successful future leaders in the company. I was in the right place at the right time, and was chosen for one of two available slots in the officer-training program.

I spent the next few years learning about banking in the executive internship program. As a trainee, I shifted from one department to another, working temporarily in all the different areas. For instance, I worked perhaps three months in trust, then the next three months in credit, and so on. The program was somewhat unstructured, since no one seemed to know what to do with the first two female banking interns! The two of us fashioned our own methods of handling things as we went along.

My training resulted in an excellent starting position with the treasury management division, a new high-profile area of the bank. Although I found it interesting, I wasn't sure if this would be a long-term career. One thing led to another, a few years went by, and my areas of responsibility expanded. Judge Hughes kept up with us, pleased to see the bank training capable females as future leaders. From modest beginnings, women have played more and more prominent roles in the industry. I am proud of the progress women have made, but there is still a considerable preponderance of men in executive leadership roles.

Early in my banking career, I might have chosen another avenue. I could have married and raised a family. I could have migrated to a different career, another state. My profession was demanding, with a great deal of travel, and I believe, in some ways, it chose me as much as I chose it. I will never know if fate directed me to take the path I did because of the connection it would ultimately have with my cancer. I only know which path I took and where it led.

Banking eventually hooked me, and my career took form. I was promoted to a first level officer, and then to assistant vice president. I loved seeing that "vice president" in my name. I would cover the word "assistant" with my finger, and imagine having the full vice president title. What would that be like? How would my life change if and when I achieved that success? What challenges would I need to surmount? What rewards waited for me to savor?

It was not only an exciting and stimulating time in my life, but also in banking. During the 1980s, deregulation, technology, and geographic expansion combined to create aggressive competition in the field. Suddenly, banks were trying to grab their share of the market. They desperately needed to distinguish themselves in the public eye, because all banks' services were basically the same, or, as the saying in the industry went, "all money is green." This fresh, dynamic activity invigorated me, and I plunged into the new competitiveness. We no longer waited for clients to come to us. We were constantly out in the market, making presentations, letting the public know what the bank had to offer. Providing solutions and consulting with corporate clients appealed to my analytical mind. I thrived on finding ways not only to meet, but to exceed, my clients' expectations. It was a challenging and hectic period, but also very enjoyable and satisfying.

In 1983, I earned that third stripe and became a full vice president of the company! My friends and I drank martinis to celebrate my promotion. That night, as I was driving home, I glanced in my rearview mirror and saw a cat flying through the air. I did a double take, chiding myself for that last martini. I was horrified to realize that someone in the car behind me had tossed a cat out the window. I turned the car around and went back.

There by the road, abandoned, was a beautiful Siamese kitten, no more than eight weeks old. Of course, I had to take her home, but I had always had dogs—big sturdy boxers. I didn't think one could trust a cat, and had no intention of keeping her. Once at home, though, I began to watch her and imagine what I would name her, if I did keep her. Finally, I said, "I guess if I'm a VP, you can be one, too."

These were the years one dreams of when embarking on a challenging new career. As I joined the corporate inner circle, I could see my ideas shaping policies. I knew that my thoughts mattered, that my voice contributed to the company's success. I managed a weighty portfolio of corporate clients. Calling on different companies allowed me to learn about a variety of businesses and to meet fascinating people. I enjoyed what I was doing, and I believed in the company.

Beyond these intangible rewards, the financial compensation began to grow. Now, in addition to a salary, I earned generous stock options, as well as incentive payments for becoming a "top performer" among my peers.

I have always pushed myself to excel in whatever I do. I flourished in this "meritocracy" corporate environment, where "pay for performance" reigned, and returns were based on merit. No one's background mattered, yet no one was paid merely for showing up. We had to book new business, and not just any transaction. It had to be good business, priced to yield profit. When the banking industry was deregulated, banks could no longer give services away free of charge. We were not a volunteer organization. We were a corporate entity, responsible to our board of directors and shareholders, committed to generate a profit and post dividends like any other business.

Many people in the general public didn't understand this at first, and resented having to pay for banking services. I learned how to sell value and to provide solutions for my clients, how to improve operating cash flow and free up funds to pay down loans or to invest. In effect, I sold solutions to corporate problems, and my clients were willing to pay for that.

These years were not only fine professionally, but also privately. Finally reaping some of the financial benefits of my ten years of dedication and hard work, I bought a charming ranch-style house in North Dallas. I chose this particular home not only for its easy accessibility to airports, restaurants, and my downtown office, but also because I foresaw how well it could serve as a place for my many good friends to congregate. Now I had a swimming pool in the backyard and a Cadillac in the garage! I commenced remodeling and furnishing my new home with a

Southwestern flair, which reflected my love for Santa Fe, New Mexico. Over the years, the flow of the rooms and the openness of the kitchen have made a natural gathering place for friends and family, generating a host of shared memories: laughter, tales told, consolation given, and mysteries solved, often over a bottle of wine and a fine meal.

My prosperity also enabled me to satisfy my passion for travel in more exotic ways. If there was a mountain in the western part of North America, it had my name on it. As an avid downhill skier, I was determined to experience the challenges of the finest ski resorts in Colorado, Utah, New Mexico, California, Nevada, Wyoming, and western Canada. As much as I delighted in the speed, the freedom, the exhilaration of skiing, I equally revered the ethereal quality of the landscape. I remember saying to a friend one time, "I don't understand how anyone can question the presence of God when they view the majesty of His creations." I was struck by the smallness of "me" relative to the mountains, which contrasted with my certainty that I, and every human, was a unique creation of God, eternally cared for and protected by Him.

I was a thirty-nine-year-old woman: healthy, athletic, outgoing, and involved. I had energy to spare, and I was leading an extremely active and rewarding life.

To dispose a soul to action we must upset its equilibrium.

~Eric Hoffer

Then, very suddenly, life changed for me. I noticed a sore walnut-sized lump in my left breast. I didn't initially pay much attention to it, because I had fibrocystic breasts, a benign condition which causes variable lumpiness and pain. Always one to self-medicate, I rubbed it with BenGay for a week or two, hoping the lump would disappear. Although I wasn't particularly suspicious of it, to be prudent, I decided to have it checked out.

I'll never forget that September day. I went to the doctor in the afternoon, and he suggested a mammogram. It was much less routine for women to have mammograms at the time, and I had never had one. After the technician made the film, she looked at me nervously, then back at the mammogram. I asked, "Is everything okay?"

She said, "Wait here a minute." She left, taking the films for the radiologist's review. A few minutes later, she returned and told me they needed to take more films.

Trying to pry more information out of the tech, I ventured, "That's kind of a large lump."

She answered, "Yes, it is." I didn't get any more details at the time, but they urged me to go to my doctor on Monday.

I met my brother for dinner that night. He lives in Fort Worth where he has a successful dental practice, but he was in Dallas for a dental society meeting. I didn't know what to make of my experience with the mammogram, and I remember saying to him during our meal, "You won't believe what happened to me this afternoon." I described the incident to him. At the time, we didn't know of any history of cancer in my family (although I have since found that one of my great aunts had breast cancer), and we agreed that the suggestion to see my doctor was surely just a precaution.

I was somewhat nervous over the weekend, but didn't allow myself to dwell too much on the possibilities. On Monday, I went to my doctor, who recommended seeing a surgeon. I asked why. His only answer was, "Well, because I'd like to have a surgeon take a look at you."

I went to the surgeon the same day, as I recall, and the surgeon said, "I think we need to biopsy this."

"You're kidding," I said. "You really think there might be a problem?"

He told me that he didn't think so, but to be on the safe side, since it was a rather large lump, he wanted to schedule a biopsy in the next few days. I can still hear the question I asked next, and the irony of those words:

"Will it leave a scar?"

2:

THREAT OF PAIN

So remember this principle when
something threatens to cause
you pain: the thing itself was no
misfortune at all; to endure it and
prevail is great good fortune.

~Marcus Aurelius

The results of the biopsy shocked me and stunned friends and family. The surgeon came to the recovery room and told me that things had not gone the way we wished. The diagnosis needed confirmation by a pathologist, but he felt sure that the tumor was malignant. I was at a loss. I couldn't begin to absorb the news. I had never dealt with cancer in my family or friends and had never been associated with any such experiences. I asked, "How could this be?"

I had made certain that the releases I signed before surgery allowed removal of the lump only on the day of the biopsy. They admitted me to the hospital, as was routine at that time, and evaluated me to determine if the cancer had metastasized, or spread, outside the breast. They found no cancer elsewhere, and suggested a mastectomy as the only viable treatment option. Nowadays the surgical treatment of breast cancer usually includes the option of removal of the tumor only, with a rim of normal tissue, but at that period of time, and with the large size of the lump, my doctors recommended aggressive surgery.

I am somewhat exacting, and I require symmetry and precision in my life. For example, my signature looks like printing, and people have sometimes seen it and protested, "No, we need your signature." Thus, I could not imagine the imbalance of having only one breast, especially a fairly large one since I was well endowed. I asked the doctor how we might address this. He sent a remarkable plastic surgeon to my room, who drew pictures all over me and showed me how we could repair the damage. He suggested using an implant for reconstruction on the left and doing a breast reduction on the right, to help equalize the two sides. It would take a few months, but he assured me that we could get Humpty Dumpty back together again.

I agreed to have the mastectomy, with the idea that we would do the reconstruction. In the span of a few short days, I had gone from a healthy, active businesswoman at the top of my game, to facing a life-threatening disease and a grim surgery. I was dealing with it all in a rush, and quite naturally, I told everyone at the bank what was happening.

I remember clearly that I was released from the hospital on Friday for a "weekend pass" before I was to be readmitted for my mastectomy the next week. My friends gathered around me. They brought food—and drink. For two days, we sat by the pool, eating, drinking, talking it out, celebrating the fact that my cancer had not spread, and commiserating the impending loss of a significant part of my body. We cried. We laughed. We toasted the tit. All in all, it was a worthy send off for my left breast.

I returned to the hospital and underwent a mastectomy on September 24. The surgeon had a pressure wrap all the way around my chest. Mummified as I was, I couldn't see anything of my shape. I had many visitors, including family, friends, and business associates from the bank. They brought beautiful flowers and lots of well wishes. It was an out-of-body experience that I observed from a distance, as if someone else were going through it.

I remember the first night after surgery. A friend stayed late with me, and I was sitting up in a chair, talking. The staff had marveled that I'd been so chipper and upbeat, visiting with people all day. A nurse tiptoed into my room and said, "Kay, I hate to bother you. Please tell me if this is an imposition, but there's a patient next door who moved here from Houston, and she's all alone. She's lost her job and has no insurance. She just found out she's got breast cancer, and she's scheduled for a mastectomy in the morning. You seem to be doing so well. Would you consider visiting with her for a minute?"

I said I would be happy to, that maybe I could encourage her. I went next door and talked with the woman for a while, trying to be as consoling as I could. As I turned to leave, I caught sight of my image in her mirror and I scared myself! I couldn't believe it! I hadn't seen my appearance all day, as I had spoken with one visitor after another. My shoulder hunched forward, my hair was mashed and matted, and I was pale as a ghost. I returned to my room, chuckling to myself. The friend waiting in my room seemed rather taken aback that I would be laughing under the circumstances, and asked why.

"I must have scared that poor woman to death," I said. "I told her she had nothing to worry about, because tomorrow at this time, she'd be just like me!"

At any rate, my visit did seem to provide the woman some comfort. From time to time, I've wondered how her story played out. The incident made a lasting impression on me because encouraging her actually made me feel better. I've never forgotten that feeling, a kind of personal healing I experienced when I reached out to another individual. The incident ignited within me a desire to help others—to offer what inspiration, strength, and hope my own life encounters could provide.

One of the sharpest memories of my stay (back then one remained in the hospital for a week) is the wonderful, compassionate care I received from delightful Irish nurses. Every morning, one of them would hold a cup of fresh, hot coffee under my nose to let the aroma wake me. All day long, they would bring me special little treats. I think I must have been somewhat of a novelty among their patients because of my youth and my upbeat attitude. I didn't consciously think about ways one could handle such a situation. I merely did what works for me—focusing on the positive news that my cancer had not spread. Although it was a large tumor, it was limited to the breast, and I felt extremely fortunate not to face the prospect of radiation or chemotherapy.

Back then, they actually referred to cure once in a while. I foresaw my experience as a mere tick mark ten years down the road. I imagined it was possible to breeze on through life, with everything back to normal. I would deal with the reconstruction and life would be good. When the doctor came in that last day, though, and he unwrapped the pressure bandage, my first look at my strangely altered body dazed me. My long-time nurse friend, Jan Meyers, or as I like to call her, "Nurse Meyers," was with me that day. I am forever grateful to her reinforcing presence, which braced me against what I saw.

Unsettled as I was though, I remember thinking, "Well, Kay, look at it this way. What about people who have to have a leg amputated, or an arm, or they lose their sight? What about those things which are more obvious to the outside world? Even though the asymmetry appalled me, I knew that plastic surgery and time could repair it. I was thankful that my future looked bright.

I returned home to convalesce a little longer. My cat, VP, helped entertain me, and she even provided me with a challenge to focus upon. My dogs had always known how to sit and shake hands. I wondered if it were possible to teach a cat that trick. I would hold treats before her and command, "Shake!" During that time of my recovery, she did learn to wave her paw in the air—more of

> *All spiritual interests are supported by animal life.*
>
> ~George Santayana

a high-five than a shake, but an astonishing sight just the same. From that time on, she always managed to amuse my friends with the greeting when they visited.

My dear friends—my angel corps—took care of meals, errands, doctor visits, and most importantly, me! Being single as I am, these faithful friends have become an extension of family and a powerful support system throughout my life. Over the years, we have all helped each other through tough times, but I believe that I have received more from them than I could ever give back.

I remember taking long, long walks, just to keep moving. I would walk four or five miles every day, always with a goal in mind. I wasn't cleared to drive yet, and I walked wherever I needed to go: to the grocery store, to take care of an errand, to sit at a café and enjoy a cup of coffee. I was also restoring myself mentally, drinking in the peacefulness and beauty of nature and the world around me. Autumn is my favorite time of year, and the weather was beautiful. Such extreme trauma had happened to me so very rapidly, and I needed to adjust, to counterbalance it, to "re-center." I saw the changes in myself reflected in the changing seasons, and I found comfort.

I focused my mind and activities on healing as quickly as possible. My doctors expected to have to wait a couple of months for my first round of reconstructive surgery, possibly starting after the first of the year. I was eager to get to that phase. Blessed with the help of friends and family, after a couple of weeks, I went back to work.

3:

CHOOSE NOT HARM

Choose not to be harmed—
and you won't feel harmed.

Don't feel harmed—
and you haven't been.

~Marcus Aurelius

W hat was interesting about my first day back at work was that no one looked me in the eye. Everybody focused on my chest. People would say hello, and then their eyes would drift because they were imagining what wasn't there. My face had a healthy glow, slightly suntanned from my long walks, and I was proud of the way I looked. But no one paid quite enough attention to Kay's face, or her eyes, or her expression, or what she was saying. Everyone was looking for what was not right about Kay instead of what was.

The curiosity and the surreptitious glances weren't the worst of it, though. The sympathetic head tilts, the whispers of, "Poor Kay," were the real killers. I don't wish to be ungracious about compassion and kindness demonstrated by others. I merely want to point out that expressions of sympathy can easily become patronizing, that pity is tinged with contempt. I hated how the lamenting made me feel—substandard, below par, like damaged goods. I remember thinking, "I've got a long way to go to overcome this, to be in a position where my colleagues will take me and what I have to say seriously again."

That next year was a bit of a blur. I put a lot of hours into my work, and I put a lot of hours into me. The first part of my reconstruction was the placement of a tissue expander on the side of my mastectomy. This procedure required me to visit the doctor weekly, in order for him to inject the expander with a saline solution. As the volume of the expander increased, the overlying skin gradually extended to accommodate it.

During this time, I had reduction surgery on my remaining breast to make its size more comparable with the future implant. Once the skin over the tissue expander had grown enough, placement of the implant required another surgery. Then I underwent yet another surgery for skin grafting and nipple reconstruction. Over time, my doctor proved his claim of being able to put Humpty Dumpty back together again!

I remember as I left the plastic surgeon's office on my final visit, I thought about the substantial and permanent changes my body had undergone during the past year. I don't believe I realized what infinitesimal increments of change were also occurring in my soul. Day by day, hour by hour, minute by minute, first the body and then the spirit evolved into a stronger, more determined Kay—a Kay resolved to overcome this setback, to prove her health, to prove her wholeness.

Everything went smoothly for about a year after the completion of my reconstruction, and then I had my first fire drill. That's the way I've come to think of the flurry of medical tests, exams, and speculation that follows any suspicious finding in a cancer survivor. After twenty years of living with cancer, I've had my share of fire drills.

The first one occurred because of a mass in my pelvis.

Shocked, I signed a consent form that listed the reason for surgery as possible breast cancer, metastatic to the uterus or ovaries. I was scared to death. It had been less than two years since I'd had my breast cancer diagnosis, a very critical time period for a cancer survivor. There was no choice but to have the surgery and see what was going on. Fortunately, the good Lord smiled on me that time, and the mass turned out to be a common benign tumor of the uterus. I opted to have a hysterectomy, because, at forty, why not?

My first fire drill and my hysterectomy were not the only milestones of turning forty. It was also around this time that my life as a banker and my life as a cancer survivor intersected in a curious way that forever changed both.

Two large Dallas banks located only a few blocks apart were major competitors. One had a portfolio based primarily on real estate lending, and it was sinking fast. Its neighbor down the street had done a tremendous amount of energy lending, and those loans were also going south. Grasping at straws, the two banks decided to get married—or in corporate terms, merge their operations—into one legal entity. I remember the *Wall Street Journal* describing the situation as two drunks trying to hold each other up. For about a year after the merger, they did a wobbly dance, but inevitably fell over.

My resume includes having been a part of that gargantuan bank failure, one of the largest in banking history. What my resume doesn't specify, though, is that the merger generated a watershed in the course of my life. When these two neighboring banks similar in size and operation joined forces, there were now two people for each available position.

My first game of corporate musical chairs began. Everyone was going round and round, and when the music stopped, there were only enough chairs for half of them. Happily for me, I still had a chair—and moreover, when I looked around at who was left, I saw something I hadn't expected. Many of the people who had come to visit me in the hospital, who knew about my mastectomy, were gone. As time passed, fewer and fewer of my co-workers knew about my situation. Then, when our merged bank failed, a North Carolina bank bought us.

I was fortunate enough to survive the second merger and join a new cast of players. The people in North Carolina surely didn't know Kay Holleman or what had happened to her. People were interested at last in what Kay had to say, and no longer looked at her as damaged goods. The out-of-state bank was looking for proven performers with deep roots in Texas. It was an important public relations move to place strong local talent on the newly created leadership team and charge them with running the Texas bank. This was the break I had been hoping for. I was rapidly given increasing areas of responsibility in the treasury management division—from running the Dallas office, to managing the North Texas region, and finally to being appointed the treasury management executive for the state of Texas.

It was around this time, with my professional and personal life running smoothly, that I lost my father. Dad deeply influenced my thinking, my perceptions, and my way of experiencing life. He loved a good time, a good joke, a good drink, and a great meal. I credit my business acumen and my sense of humor directly to him, and my physical resemblance to him is striking as well. His family was the most important part of his life. I must admit that from a very early age, I knew I was the "apple of his eye." He was in Okinawa when I was born. He used to say that he missed my first nine months, and spent the rest of his life making it up to me.

Sidney A. Holleman, Sr. came from a long line of self-made, successful southern Louisianans. They were passionate, genteel people who honored family ties above all, found fun and humor everywhere, and thrived on mouthwatering southern delicacies. Dad taught me to enjoy many of the finer things in life early. One of my favorite childhood recollections is an image of myself at eight years old, sitting at Dad's side in a famous oyster bar in New Orleans. We made frequent trips to New Orleans in order for him to indulge in repasts at favorite restaurants. We would always begin the evening with "a dozen on the half-shell." I still enjoy that ritual, and I think of him fondly when I do.

Dad died of a heart attack at the age of seventy-six, in 1987, three years after my initial cancer diagnosis. Although my illness had shocked and saddened him, it didn't take him long to realize that I was going to stand up and fight. We shared a strong,

Never the spirit is born/The spirit will cease to be never/ Never the time when it was not. End and beginning are dreams/Birthless and deathless and changeless/Remains the spirit forever. Death has not touched it at all/Dead though the house of it seems.

~Sioux Prayer of Passing

loving father-daughter bond, as well as a similar resilient nature. He saw me face cancer and survive it the first time. I'm sure he knows now that I've done it more than once.

It's important to note that I never thought of myself as a cancer patient. Rather, I was someone who had had a malignant tumor, and now the tumor was removed—gone. I stayed mentally and physically active, reinforcing the fact that the cancer was an isolated event of my past. I've always demanded perfection from myself in whatever I do. There was no way I could reconcile being sick with perfection, so I "moved on down the road."

I bought a high-performance, lightweight, compact bicycle and started going to rallies all over Texas. I would load the bike onto my car, and strike out on a Saturday at six o'clock in the morning, listening to my classical music, driving to some small town where a bike rally was scheduled. Then I would get on that bicycle and ride sixty, seventy-five, a hundred miles.

What my body could do—if I pushed it and trained it enough—amazed me. As I rode through East Texas piney woods, West Texas plains, or the central Texas hill country, I would repeat my mantra: "I am healthy, I am healthy, I am healthy."

I had always been active, athletic; I was a tennis player in college. But now I became passionate, almost obsessive, about my fitness. I trained for two years in preparation for a 680-mile bicycle trip along the west coast of New Zealand's South Island. A San Francisco-based company, one of the finest active travel companies in the world, offered the trip. Our group consisted of twenty-five bikers from all over the US, ranging in age from thirty to seventy. Doctors, lawyers, bankers, professors, and executives participated in this grand three-week journey.

We rode across deserted beaches along the magnificent Tasman Sea. We saw sheep farms butting up against rainforests, alpine peaks with breathtaking vistas, and imposing waterfalls. We cycled past forest-lined lakes and through lush river valleys. We crossed the New Zealand Alps, biking over a passage at an altitude of 10,500 feet. We rode uphill for days and then downhill for days. Once we completed a "century ride"—a hundred miles in one day.

The rigors of the journey quickly sorted us into categories of faster or slower cyclists. I wasn't in the uppermost tier, but my methodical training served me well, and I found myself in the faster half of the group. I was impressed with the way we all bonded. The stronger riders consistently bolstered and cheered on those who fell behind and may otherwise have been lost to the "sag-wagon." As we gathered each evening at inns along the way, the discouraged stragglers may well have given up if not for the encouragement from others. My interaction with such a collaborative band gratified me and deepened my overall experience.

With each new day, my breath caught at the limitless splendor of the landscape. The spectacular beauty and the diverse topography awed me. Some of our group went bungee-jumping into the Kawarau River Gorge. Since one recent brush with death was enough for me, I did not bungee jump off the bridge! However, I did enjoy white-water rafting down the Buller River. I also hired a small seaplane and took a scenic flight to Milford Sound, New Zealand's most famous fjord. Another adventure was exploring the dazzling Franz Josef Glacier by helicopter and on foot.

Into every empty corner, into all forgotten things and nooks, Nature struggles to pour life, pouring life into the dead, life into life itself.

~Henry Beston

The allure of the scenery and the genuine hospitality of the people made my trip to New Zealand one of the unforgettable events of my life.

When I finished the trip, I can't describe the sense of accomplishment, the sense of health, the sense of vitality I felt. I believed I could accomplish almost anything. I continued cycling on weekends, still pushing, training, repeating my mantra. It was a joyful and promising time. I continued to travel, taking biking trips to the California wine country (combining two of my passions), and to Vermont in autumn. Other favorite biking expeditions included touring Virginia, the Shenandoah Valley, Mississippi, and the Louisiana bayous, viewing antebellum mansions, and delving into Civil War history. With every healthy year that went by, I felt more and more as if I were going to be in the "you are a cure" statistics.

Five cancer-free years turned into six, then seven and eight. I was in my late forties and had been evaluated carefully year after year, with no recurrence of cancer. I thought I had beaten it, and I began to think less and less about it. Although a cancer survivor can never vanquish the idea entirely, I no longer thought of my cancer many times a day as I had in the beginning. The further I got away from the initial diagnosis, the less often it would creep into my mind at night, or early in the morning, or when I had a little down time.

When thoughts of my cancer did cross my mind, the impact tended to be more positive than negative. It reminded me of a statement I had read by Elisabeth Kübler-Ross: "It's only when we truly know and understand that we have a limited time on earth—and that we have no way of knowing when our time is up, we will then begin to live each day to the fullest, as if it was the only one we had." In other words, I was thinking more in terms of how to live than of how to die.

My banking career thundered onward. At least seven more mergers had occurred, and every time, my responsibilities grew. By nine years after my cancer diagnosis, I had become a senior vice president, the southwest region treasury management executive, and had several states reporting to me: Texas, Oklahoma, New Mexico, Arizona, and Nevada. The more I handled, the bigger the personal and financial rewards I reaped. Furthermore, I was making an impact as a leader in the company.

My personal philosophy dictated pay for performance, incentive-based compensation, and hiring only the best. I surrounded myself with smart, decisive, intuitive individuals, paid them extremely well, and coached them to higher and higher standards of performance. It paid off. I gained a reputation for recruiting, developing, and retaining "A-players." In a corporate world of constant change, I was able to keep key talent for our company.

I also felt that the more power I had, the more I gave away. Nobody worked for me; everyone worked with me. Our teamwork consistently resulted in our recognition as the top performing team in the nation. Going to work every day was enjoyable for me. I loved the company and its culture.

I was careful never to speak of my prior illness at work. Although I remained silent about my own major life crisis, I was always sensitive to others' suffering and made a point to support those who were going through troubled times. I must have demonstrated a fair amount of compassion, because many times they would say, "You understand these things so well. How is that?" I would reply with some appropriate evasion such as, "Because I lost my mother early in life and experienced health problems with her for three years."

I want to make it clear that I did not experience overt discrimination at the bank. The reason I kept my past quiet was that I never wanted to expose myself again to that look in people's eyes.

It's a look telling you that whether or not they mean to, they are discounting you. They are disregarding you or minimizing you in some way because you have an illness or you had an illness or you have only one breast, or an amputated leg, or diabetes, or you're deaf, or blind, or fat. People often dwell on the weaknesses or flaws in others, sometimes unintentionally, and perhaps even subconsciously. But whether it's done on purpose or not, society often cruelly relegates the person with an infirmity to a substandard status.

I think part of this subtle prejudice is due to misunderstanding the overall effects of a major experience like cancer, or having a mastectomy or an amputation. Others often don't grasp how one can deal with cancer; they don't see that one manages cancer much like any other problem in life. You can still be happy if you've had cancer. You can still be happy if you have only one breast or one leg. Happiness is a choice; it's not some gift magically bestowed. I am responsible for making myself happy. Although I didn't give myself cancer, I chose the way I dealt with it.

I decided when I first got sick that my version of the serenity prayer, which has kept me sane, would be this: "It is what it is. There's no getting around that in life, and whatever 'it' is, we make the most of it. There are things we can't control in life, but we have to do our part to control those things we can." In my case, I couldn't control getting a cancer diagnosis, but I could control my behavior after that diagnosis. I could do everything in my power to stay healthy. I could exercise, watch my diet, drink in moderation, build up my immune system, and avoid smoking.

I'm convinced that life is 10 percent what happens to me and 90 percent how I react to it. Someone once said, "It's good to have an end to journey towards, but it is the journey that matters in the end." I've said before many times, and

I'll say it right now: having cancer was the best thing that ever happened to me. Having cancer has helped me grow tremendously as a person—as a compassionate, understanding human being.

Having cancer has helped me live life thoroughly, but I was not going back to talking about it openly in the professional realm. The day I looked up and the people who knew about my past health issues were gone, was a happy day for me.

In 1994, I was ten years out from my initial cancer diagnosis. For each of those years, I had undergone annual bone scans, liver scans, and other tests that cancer survivors have. Even after ten years, at forty-nine, I was still nervous about the procedures, but I would say to myself, "Kay, you're having your tests so the doctors can prove what we already know, and what we know is that you're healthy. We're not looking to find cancer, but affirming the fact that you're enjoying great health." And so it was that my ten-year anniversary found me cancer-free.

The next year, when I went in for my annual tests, the doctor said, "After ten years, we don't need to do these scans anymore. You've beaten the odds."

It was like cutting the umbilical cord, and it made me nervous that suddenly I was going to fly solo, with just a regular internist, like everybody else, and no annual scans. I asked, "Don't you think we could do the scans anyway?"

But of course, it was also a splendid day to hear the words, "You've been cancer-free for eleven years, and that means you're okay. So go and be happy." And I did, and I was, and I thanked the good Lord.

At the time of my first cancer diagnosis, the doctors set ten years as a milestone. Two years were great, five were fabulous, and at ten, they said, you went into the cure column. I remember thinking, "Ten years—I'll be almost fifty!" But the time went by rather quickly. So after my eleventh-year doctor visit, I went out and celebrated, something I've always done with panache. I love to celebrate. Life is a celebration. Why shouldn't it be? I went out with friends and toasted a momentous decade plus one year. It had passed without any cancer recurring, and now life was going to become for me what it was for anybody else who had never been diagnosed with cancer.

4:

THAT WHICH IS ROUSED

The mind is that which is roused and directed by itself. It makes of itself what it chooses. It makes what it chooses of its own experience.

~Marcus Aurelius

It was the spring of 1996, and I had been playing a lot of golf, riding my bicycle, working hard, and feeling great. I noticed what I thought was a pulled pectoral muscle on my left upper chest. After a week or so with no improvement, I went to the doctor. He didn't think it was anything serious, but as a precaution, he suggested that a surgeon examine me. I grew a bit more anxious as the surgeon ordered a sonogram, MRI, and CAT scan, but I still felt fairly confident that it wasn't a major problem. At length, the doctors recommended surgery, a biopsy, to see exactly what was going on around the clavicle and pectoral muscle above the implant.

I'd been cancer-free for almost twelve years. The biopsy diagnosis dropped like a bombshell.

It's difficult to describe the shock and disbelief and frustration I experienced when they told me that once again, I had a malignancy. I thought it must surely have nothing to do with my first cancer because of the long interval between occurrences, but the doctor said, "Yes, it is a recurrence of your initial breast cancer."

When my cancer first appeared in 1984, it had not spread to lymph nodes. Now I had cancer in lymph nodes above the implant and under my left arm. Extensive surgery would be required in the axillary, or underarm area. I remember hoping that the surgery wouldn't disrupt the implant, because I had been very happy with it and didn't want to go through a replacement procedure.

Within days, I underwent surgery to remove the second malignancy. The pathologist found cancer in three lymph nodes, and invasion of soft tissue. I resented that this situation could happen after I'd come so far—after my relentless effort to

fortify myself physically, mentally, and emotionally. A recurrence was a stinging slap in the face.

I was still in the hospital when another thing
happened that would change my life forever. My
brother was visiting me, and I was silently angry,
yet also shaken. I must admit I was feeling very
sorry for myself. It was then that a delightful female
oncologist came into the room to meet me. She
radiated self-confidence and warmth. She walked
over and looked me straight in the eye, engaging
me instantly. I felt encouraged and reassured by
her strength. She sat down on the side of the bed,
and I said, "This is serious, isn't it?"

"Yes, it is serious," she said. "It's unusual to
have a recurrence after twelve years, especially
when there was no lymph node involvement the
first time—but that's what has happened." At this
point in time, I didn't know what that meant.

"Is this something that can be treated?" I
asked.

"Yes, it can be treated."

"Successfully treated?" I pressed.

"Yes, I believe it can." She said. Then she explained that the treatment would involve approximately six months of chemotherapy, followed by six weeks of radiation. The treatment would be very aggressive because having cancer in the bloodstream, lymphatic system, or a major organ requires extreme measures.

I remember looking at her and saying, "When can we start?" It would be four to six weeks, giving me time to heal. They also needed to check for cancer elsewhere and to implant a port for injection of the chemotherapy drugs.

Maybe all along I had hidden suspicions that my cancer had returned, because this time I hadn't told anyone at the bank what was happening to me. In fact, I decided that no matter what was going on with my health, I wouldn't let anyone at the bank know. I was now a senior vice president of the company, and my boss was in a different city. I, therefore, had enough flexibility that I was able to have surgery on a Friday and be back at work on Tuesday with no one the wiser.

A few days after I learned what type of treatment I would have, I was visiting my brother.

A Wounded Deer—leaps highest.

~Emily Dickinson

I told him that I didn't know how I would manage because my hair would fall out, and wigs always looked unnatural. My brother told me he had heard of wigs made of human hair, with each strand pulled through individually, creating a completely natural look.

"You need to investigate that quickly," he said, "because you've only got a month or so before you start the chemotherapy. Maybe you could even have a wig made from your own hair."

I thought it was a marvelous idea. I did some research and found a place that made human hair wigs. It would take about a month, so I went in right away. They taped all my hair down, cut some of it off for the wig, and then plastered a form around my head for exact measurements. Sure enough, about a month later, I had an absolutely believable-looking human hair wig!

Day surgery was required for insertion of the chemotherapy port. I remember saying to my oncologist at the time, "I'm not going to tell anyone at the bank about this."

"You're not?" She sounded incredulous.

"No," I said, "I don't think it's appropriate for me to discuss it, and it's really no one's business but my own. I've got a lot at stake, and I'm not willing to risk it. So, I'm just going to have chemotherapy, put the wig on, go to work every day, and no one will know."

She looked at me oddly and said, "I've never had anyone do that before."

"Well, I'm going to do it."

I never thought for a minute that the company I worked for would shut me out if they knew I had cancer. I was in senior management at this point, on the inside track, and there was no question that, as a business, we were benevolent, that we took good care of our associates, that we did the right thing for people. It wasn't a company policy I was worried about. It was the individuals—or more accurately, the undercurrent thoughts that would run through the minds of the individuals.

I was never again going to be viewed professionally the way I'd been viewed in 1984. I wasn't going to try to lead people who knew that I had cancer, and who would be distracted by it, wondering about my scars instead of concentrating on making a profit for the company. I didn't want to devitalize my team with worries about my health.

Those I led needed to cast their undivided

attention on driving the numbers and succeeding and developing—in short, on being the best team in the United States.

There is a tendency in human nature to sideline those with perceived frailties. It may be rooted in caring—maybe we don't want to add more stress to an already burdened life—but the end result is that we can be guilty of putting others aside. I wasn't willing to risk that. I was a single, professional, career woman, a senior executive with one of the largest financial institutions in the world. I didn't have anyone else to rely upon. What if I took the risk and found out I was right? What if all anyone could focus on was that Kay had cancer twice? And when was she going to pass on? I was a very aggressive, healthy looking, successful person. People paid attention to me in that context, and I didn't want to change my entire image with the words, "I have cancer."

My doctor had a warning for me, though. She

said, "Do it if you can, but you're going to miss the nurturing and the whole support system that people who know your situation can provide."

"Doctor," I said, "I don't need that. I need my career, and I need the life I've built for myself. I need to feel I'm making a contribution, and I need to feel successful. What I don't need is to think about being a sick chemo patient."

She smiled and said, "Well, let's give it a shot."

Thus began one of the most daring rounds in my escapades of keeping cancer in the closet. I became quite inventive, which in this case is a euphemism for deceptive. I cringe now at the thought of how many evasions, half-truths, and downright lies I came up with. In all other ways, I am an honest and forthright person. My parents raised me as a Catholic with twelve years of parochial school, trained by the sisters and brothers of St. Mary. The first public education I ever had was my college coursework. I often wonder what the good nuns and brothers would think if they knew that I could look anyone in the eye and say I was going to a meeting, when I was really going to have a radiation treatment. But preventing others from knowing about my circumstances strained my frankness beyond its limits, and I did what I had to do to protect myself.

The first challenge was to come up with a reasonable explanation for being out during my initial chemotherapy. One presented itself fairly readily. I am an avid traveler. Instead of a lot of little vacations, I like the big bang, to really get away from it all. I was never one of those senior leaders at a company who thought the business would fall apart if I wasn't there. My philosophy is that if it did fall apart, you probably weren't doing a very good job. I had hard-working, capable people on my team, and I developed them fully, never hesitating to delegate responsibilities. It was my habit to take an annual three-week

European vacation. I simply told my teammates that I was taking my usual trip, and naturally, no one gave it a second thought. Instead of Europe, I was starting treatment with Adriamycin and Cytoxan, two very powerful chemotherapeutic drugs. A day or two after the first treatment, my hair began to slip a bit, and within a couple of weeks, it was falling out in big clumps.

My wig had been slow to come in, but at last it arrived, and I went to pick it up. I remember sitting in the chair and asking the owner of the company with whom I'd been working to shave my head.

"Why?" he asked. "You still have hair."

I said, "Because we know it's going to come out, and I don't want to watch it happen. Just shave it off, and I'll put the wig on, and then in a few days I'll go back to work."

So that's what he did, and that's what I did.

I was nervous about going back to work, but

I was also still angry. I believe anger, more than anything else, fueled me at that point. Maybe rage wasn't such a bad thing, because it drove me to fix things instead of falling down and playing dead. I'll never forget the day I went back to work. I tripped and fell going out my back door, and tore a hole in my shin. That event was traumatic in itself, but I finally gathered myself and trudged on to work, limping a little. I remember thinking, "I wonder if I can pull this off."

I made the effort to walk into the office with a strong gait, standing tall and carrying myself proudly. What happened next was unexpected. My associates greeted me with questions such as, "Did you have a nice trip to Europe, Kay?" Two or three people looked at my hair and said, "Oh, gee, your hair is a little different—looks good." Then they went on about their business. During the day, another one or two people mentioned my new hairstyle, and that was the end of that.

I thought others would focus on me, and take in all the details. It turned out that what they perceived was my overall manner: how I walked, how I carried myself, what I had to say—not what my hair looked like. By the end of that day, I was quite encouraged. No one noticed. No one fixated on Kay's hair, as I had feared. I went home thinking, "I can do this."

I began to salvage the bad train wreck of recurrent cancer, to take charge of the part of my life that I could control. Even though I couldn't manipulate fate and avoid having a recurrence, I could protect my livelihood: my career. I jumped into the "act" with both feet. Learning how to maintain my secret was an adventure. I didn't want anyone looking down the back of my neck—literally. If there's anywhere that a wig looks artificial, it's around the neckline, especially with the short hairstyle I had. I worked in a seventy-two-story building, and when I entered an elevator, I always stepped to the back. That way no one had a view of my neckline. When I was leading a meeting, I always sat with my back to the wall for the same reason.

The wig became such an important part of my life that I named it. I chose to call it "Sybil" after the story of the woman with multiple personalities, because when I put Sybil on, my personality changed. I became strong. I became whole. With Sybil, there wasn't anything that would give evidence of Kay's illness. It became a joke with the close friends who knew what I was going through. If they were having me over for dinner, we would talk about whether I would invite Sybil. Often, if I just went down the street or around the corner, Sybil would get to stay home, and we'd all laugh about it.

The first day I wore Sybil into my doctor's office, she didn't know it was a wig—although as an oncologist, she sees people wearing wigs every day. My pretense impressed her, and she cheered me on. She understood what was at stake for me. Having recurrent cancer at age fifty and working as a senior executive for a large company, where would I go if they sidelined me? What was I going to do? What would happen to my insurance? What would happen to my income? What would happen to me?

Once she commented to me, "You should write a book about this some day, because I've never had a patient who handled cancer and chemotherapy the way you're handling it. I have patients that stay in bed sick when they take chemotherapy. I have patients that are so sick, they take six-month medical leaves. You're traveling. You manage twenty offices. They've promoted you again. You look, you walk, and you act like a person who feels good."

Once again, I had learned how not to be the victim but rather to take charge of a situation that was challenging. I didn't give into it. I wasn't pessimistic or sorry for myself. Instead, I thought, "It was only three lymph nodes, and this is treatable. What if it were a situation that couldn't be treated?" I counted myself lucky and forged ahead. The treatment process was just another aspect of my daily routine. Over time, I completely involved myself in my masquerade. I became so good at it that when another merger occurred, they promoted me right in the middle of chemotherapy!

I don't want to imply that absolutely no one at work knew I had recurrent cancer. In fact, there were two or three trusted inner circle colleagues with whom I worked for at least fourteen years, who had some knowledge of what I was going through. They never spoke of it, however, and I never made a general announcement.

I believe in the self-fulfilling prophecy: we are what we think we are, and we become what we think we will become. I do not think of myself as a sick person. I don't allow such thoughts. Believe me, I understand the seriousness of the situation, but I don't like for others to consider me sick. I don't want anyone's sympathy. I don't want people to look at me and say, "Isn't that a shame." I don't want people to see me and say, "I wonder how much longer she's going to make it." I am as healthy and robust as I see myself, and I see myself able-bodied and flourishing, always.

When it was time to have radiation, I went in to visit the doctor. The radiologist looked at me, then looked at my file, then looked back at me. He said, "There must be some mistake."

"Why?" I asked.

"Well, Ms. Holleman, this file says you've had six months of chemotherapy, but I see you haven't lost your hair."

Boy, did I have a good laugh with him when I told him I was wearing a wig, and I had named it Sybil! He was so impressed that he asked the nurses and others in the office to come see it. No one could believe Sybil was a wig. That day reconfirmed my confidence.

I went through six weeks of radiation, every day at four o'clock. I scheduled it late in the day, so I could go straight home from the radiation center. I will admit, after six months of chemotherapy and now beginning radiation, I was tired in the evenings. Accommodating the demands of my work was difficult, too, because the daily radiation treatment prevented me from my usual business travels. Sometimes I had to go to a dinner or an evening event with a client, and I handled it by arranging earlier evenings. I needed more rest in order to get up at five o'clock, work out on the treadmill, and get to the bank by eight o'clock. I had maintained that routine for twelve years, and treatment for cancer wasn't going to interrupt it now.

Those who knew what I was hiding, including my oncologist, were more and more astounded at the approach I chose. Much, much later, she let me know that although she has had a rare patient keep cancer hidden from family, she has never known anyone to hide cancer to the extent that I did, while maintaining, as she phrased it, "a high profile."

The fact of the matter is, I didn't know what people did when they had chemo because I'd never had chemo before, and I didn't know anyone who had. I didn't know how one was supposed to act or feel. I did know, though, how I was going to act, and how I was going to feel. I was orchestrating my future. I didn't plan to miss a beat, and I didn't.

5:

THINK OF YOURSELF AS DEAD

Think of yourself as dead.
You have lived your life.
Now take what's left and live
it properly.

~Marcus Aurelius

R ound two. That's the way I thought of my
return to work without Sybil. My treatment
for recurrent cancer was finished, and enough
time had passed for my hair to grow back. It was
the second time in my career I had undergone
cancer treatment. It was the second time I found
myself in the position of reengaging after a hitch
in my standard operating mode.

I felt as though I were crossing a threshold.
In fact, I think I was crossing more than one. I
was fifty-two years old. Somewhere around age
fifty, one finds a place of maturity and wisdom, a
place of liberation, and also a place of loss. I saw
the first of my contemporaries die over the next
few years. I observed physical changes of aging in

my friends and myself. These things reminded me of my mortality, and helped me realize that time is not endless—our individual time on earth, at least, is a finite gift.

In this phase of existence, we must admit that a major part of our life is over, but there's still something inside that aches or even demands to be born. There was a part of me that really wanted to share my experiences. I wanted to use what I had

The days come and go like muffled and veiled figures sent from a distant friendly party, but they say nothing, and if we do not use the gifts they bring, they carry them as silently away.

~Ralph Waldo Emerson

learned to help other people, other cancer patients, and other survivors. My victory over cancer excited me, and I wanted to share the triumph, to sound the trumpet, but I couldn't. More accurately, I chose not to, worrying that openness about my disease would negatively impact my career. Instead, I channeled my energy, enthusiasm, and eagerness toward my profession.

The spirit I put into my work led to the crossing of yet another threshold, that of a leader. After my second bout with cancer, I came into my own as a developer of people. I was able to motivate others to achieve higher and higher standards and goals. I generated a personal record—as well as a team record—of achievement.

In part, my drive and my zest emerged from a very real sense that I cannot take being alive for granted. My oncologist and I spoke frankly about my cancer. She was and is my partner in healthcare, and she knows I seek information and deal in facts.

"The cancer will come back, won't it?" I asked her.

She didn't try to soften it. "Yes, the cancer will come back; the only question is when."

Technically speaking, I had stage three cancer, but my doctor doesn't like to categorize the disease as such because its biologic behavior is individual, and the timing is unpredictable. We have no way of knowing how long cancer will stay in remission, or when it will become active. Hearing her words crystallized for me what living in the present moment means. We can all talk about living in the "right now," and we even know what it means intellectually, but it's another matter to apply the principle.

Until that time, planning had been a habit. Family and friends even described me as a bit obsessive or compulsive. Planning for tomorrow, for a rainy day, for the future, came naturally. The time was ripe to alter that tendency and to become aware of the moment, a very powerful concept for me. This moment is the only thing any of us has. Frequently, we squander our time . . . dwelling on the past or projecting anxiety into future possibilities. Our lives don't exist in those places, though. They exist only here and now. I am much more adept at paying attention to the present than I was in my early adulthood; just in case I forget, I have a key ring that reminds me: "Be in the moment."

I knew there were still more mergers happening at the company, and the top of the pyramid was growing smaller. I weighed that knowledge against the fact that I would, at some point in the future, have to deal with my cancer again. Thus, putting Sybil back in the closet was symbolic of more than one change in my life. From both a professional and a personal standpoint, I hit my stride between 1997 and 2001—when my cancer was back in remission, and I had a sense of urgency about life.

I am proud of what I accomplished during those years. The satisfaction I found in my working relationships was due in large part, I believe, to two concepts at the heart of my business philosophy. The first was my commitment to rewarding achievement. Although I was constantly raising the bar, I was persistent in recognizing my teammates' accomplishments. The motto "winning with friends" expresses the second idea. There was no running over others to get ahead, and there were no prima donnas on my team. Furthermore, I always believed it was authoritarian and condescending to refer to others as your employees or your staff. I saw those who worked with me as my associates and teammates, and I called them such. I led people instead of managing them. I never fell into the power trap that derails so many senior executives.

Those next five years, almost six, were exceptional for me. I immersed myself in my career and found deep fulfillment in developing others as well as myself. The ceaseless merger activity of that era in banking created constant change and unremitting tension among those caught in the flux. I think the confusion and turbulence of those times honed my confidence and clarity in dealing with complex issues. I guided my associates through one professional crisis after another, during a time when job security was in short supply. I was able to lead and motivate people while providing a sense of security in a world of chaos. The gratitude and appreciation they extended to me in turn rewarded me, motivated me, and reinforced my own commitment.

I think my professional success was directly related to my ability to manage myself, to find some degree of security and serenity in the middle of my personal chaos. Nothing ever happens to us accidentally. I think that things are determined for us by a higher power, whom I call God. I believe my role on earth—my life on earth—has had more purpose and meaning because of my cancer.

I had been dealing with cancer at this point in my life for twelve or thirteen years.

Those years from 1997 to 2001 could have been a time of surrender, a time of giving up in the face of an uncertain future. Instead, they were years of growth and learning, of reaching out to others, of achieving ever higher goals. I refused to disengage. I simply would not drop out. I rolled up my sleeves and jumped in with gusto and passion. Both my health and my career have been unpredictable and unsettled. They have taught me to be flexible and adaptable, less afraid of change and more accepting of what I cannot control. They have made me a better person.

6:

No Hold
on the Soul

Things have no hold on the soul. They have no access to it, cannot move or direct it. It is moved and directed by itself alone. It takes the things before it and interprets them as it sees fit.

~Marcus Aurelius

In 2001, I again marked a cancer-free, five-year anniversary. It had been that long since my recurrence, and it was extremely encouraging. I felt great. I was taking care of myself, exercising, and eating right. My work required a tremendous amount of travel, and I often flew three, four, five times a week to offices scattered from Houston to California. Meetings took place all over the United States and sometimes in Canada. I was in my element—working hard, playing hard, and enjoying every minute.

In the summer of 2001, I decided to do some remodeling. Things got askew, with the kitchen torn up and unusable. I basically lived in the back half of the house during the mess. Mild fatigue set in, and I attributed it to the upset of my routine. In retrospect, I may have noticed some hair loss, but nothing I couldn't explain away to myself.

Every four or five months during that entire five-year period, my oncologist had checked me over, always performing a blood test for a breast cancer marker. Although the test is not 100 percent accurate, it may detect the presence of malignant activity before any other signs or symptoms manifest.

I went in for my regularly scheduled doctor visit in early summer, and everything seemed fine. About a week later, I got a telephone call from the doctor's office, telling me that the cancer marker was slightly elevated. Although it had always fallen in the normal range since I had been in remission, the doctor wasn't particularly suspicious at this point. Things other than malignancy, including some variable factor in the specimen or its handling, can affect the test results. They instructed me to stop by at my earliest convenience to have my blood drawn again to repeat the test. I went in the next day, and they took more blood to send to the lab.

A few days later, I got another call—this time from my doctor instead the nurse. She said, "The cancer marker has gone up a little more, and I think we should do some scans, just to be sure everything is okay." I was very frightened, but I imagined that the stress of my home being in disarray may have affected the test results. I immediately scheduled the CAT scans. The first round of imaging studies showed nothing, but another measure of the cancer marker was even higher. I underwent another round of scans, including an MRI of the chest, abdomen, and brain. By then, it was September, and the cancer marker was still elevated.

I went to my doctor for the results of my latest scans. The minute she opened the door of the exam room, I knew something was wrong.

She came over, patted me on the shoulder, and sat down beside me.

"The brain scan was normal and the lung scan was normal," she said, "but the MRI of your liver indicated there was a malignancy in the right lobe." Those words, "there was a malignancy in the right lobe," were ringing in my ears, and I shook my head. I couldn't believe what I had heard.

"Doctor, this is really serious, isn't it?" I asked.

"Yes, it's really serious. Breast cancer travels through the blood to lungs and liver, bone and brain. Your liver is the filter system for the entire body; if you have cancer cells filtering through the liver, over time, you're likely to develop cancer there."

"Is this treatable?" I asked.

"Yes, it's treatable," she said. "I want to look these tests over and consult with a few people. Come back in a couple of days and we'll talk about our next steps."

I remember leaving and walking to my car

in a fog. I drove toward the bank, not knowing what to do. I was in a state of shock. Initially, I had gone twelve years and now almost six more, cancer-free. But here it was again, in the liver—a major organ—and you can't live without a liver. I pulled my car off the road, and I sat a while. Then I dialed my brother and told him what had happened. He was shaken, but I said, "I have another appointment in a couple of days, and we'll decide our treatment of choice and our action plan." He wanted to go with me, and, of course, I said I would like that very much.

After I finished speaking with him, I told myself, "You can sit here and cry and be upset and pity yourself. You can get more and more frightened and focus on the fact that this could be it—or you can drive downtown, go into the bank, get involved in something positive, and do three-fourths of your day's work." So, for whatever it was worth, I did go to work, and I did hold a few meetings. I did what I needed to do. I came home rather late that evening and did the same thing the next day. I think I actually went out of town on a business trip and then came back and went to have my meeting with the doctor and my brother.

She recommended some new drugs, which they needed to test against my DNA. I had that done, but unfortunately, the drugs would not work with my DNA. Her next recommendation was a combination of two drugs: Taxotere every three weeks through an intravenous port, followed by two weeks of Xeloda, taken orally, several times a day. You can't irradiate a liver, and thus, chemotherapy would be the course of treatment.

I knew I would have to get Sybil back out, and I would have to "go to Europe" again. I would have to get a port implanted and have chemo again, and all my hair was going to fall out once more. My work demanded a great deal, but I thought, "You know, Kay, you've done it once before, you can do it again."

When I told my doctor how I was going to handle it again, she said, "Kay, this is going to be pretty hard."

I said, "So would losing my job, and I can't risk it. I'm going to work every day, I'm going to wear Sybil, and I'm going to play the masquerade to the best of my ability. I'm going to be in the closet with this cancer again."

I was fifty-six years old at that time. I didn't want to hear that cancer had metastasized to my liver, of course, but a certain level of acceptance came much more quickly this time. I did not experience the horrendous disbelief and anger I had at my first recurrence, after being cancer-free for twelve years. At that time, I thought I had probably been cured after passing the ten-year mark.

It was different in 2001. I had known—not liked, but known—that having cancer in my blood stream and my lymphatic system meant that at some point it would return. After that, I was not considered cured, but in remission. Acceptance thus came soon, and then the fight or flight response ignited. Adrenaline started pumping, and the only thing I could think of was how to get this cancer back into remission as quickly and as aggressively as possible.

I still thought of myself as a person in good health. I believe that good health is more than the absence of disease. I think that good health manifests in high energy, emotional balance, physical strength, mental clarity, vitality, and vigor. I came into this third encounter with cancer in a state of excellent health and started off the treatment at peak physical strength. I had been working out and taking care of myself. When the doctor said this was going to be tough, I was prepared. My goal was to get the treatment behind me as quickly as possible, push the cancer back into remission, and then continue to enjoy life.

It was time for Sybil to come back out of the closet. I announced to my team that I was going to Europe. Once again, I headed off to "Europe" for three weeks, and once again, I had a port implanted in my chest and began chemo treatments. After a couple of weeks, I went back to the wigmaker and asked him to shave my head again. When my three-week "trip" was over, I put Sybil back on and nervously returned to work. People asked how the trip was, and I told them I had a wonderful time, describing in detail where I had been and what I had been doing on a vacation that never happened. One day led to the next, and I found myself pulling off a second masquerade.

It may have been impossible for me to camou-flage this series of treatments if I were managing a single office each day. Here again, though, my profession and my cancer worked in a kind of synchronicity. Dallas was my home office, but I was out of Dallas more than I was in it, because I oversaw twenty offices scattered over six different states. I may have been, for example, in Houston one day and not visited that office again for a month or six weeks. Because of the level of responsibility I had attained, I could be anywhere at any time. Having a different hairstyle was easy if only a certain group of people saw me once every month or every six weeks.

Thus, the circumstances of my work provided me with a unique opportunity to lead this double life again. I carried off my duties at the bank and carried on with my cancer treatment, without ever having to let that line intersect, without ever having to reveal myself to my teammates. I was able to manage my own schedule, to hold meetings when and where I chose, and to do conference calls connecting twenty or thirty different offices.

I want to restate how crucial it was not to have others think of me as a person in ill health. In the business culture, executives must be healthy to maintain their leadership roles. I have seen careers ravaged by the image of illness. People have health problems, and others begin to think of them, and see them as sick; after a while, the sickness becomes who and what they are. They completely lose their ability to motivate, lead, or manage because others are preoccupied with the sickness instead of interacting with the person.

If we are absolutely honest with ourselves, regardless of what policies companies have in place, we have to admit that illness impacts the way we look at people. Although it's nice to experience the support and the caring, empathy and pity are opposite sides of the same coin. I do not in any way discount mercy and grace. These characteristics help form the backbone of civilization. I only want to bring attention to the detrimental emotions that may lurk beneath sympathy.

I felt that as long as I fulfilled my responsibilities at the bank—not just in a mediocre sense, but performing at the highest levels—I was entitled to keep my cancer a secret. As long as I was handling it all, leading a team of excellence, bearing the burden, achieving the goals and the numbers, I didn't think my health concerns were anyone else's business.

I must admit that relative to the chemotherapy drugs I took the first time, this was a whole different ballgame. I have a very strong constitution and a very strong stomach, fortunately, but after three or four Taxotere rounds and the daily Xeloda, I experienced major side effects. Xeloda is an extremely powerful anti-cancer drug, but it wrought havoc with my digestive system. In addition, ulcers developed in my mouth—"fever blisters" to the general public—making it very difficult to eat. I lost five or ten pounds, but I had some to spare, and I still didn't look sick. Then my eyes began to tear. Next, my hands and feet became red and swollen and peeled painfully. I was wearing heels and business suits to work, and I had to rest my feet when I could. Many times, I sat in my office with the door closed, my shoes off, and my feet propped up. The fact that it was winter gave me an excuse to wear gloves. Otherwise, I often concealed my hands in my pockets.

All of this, of course, made it much harder to carry out the plan, and it stretched my physical endurance to the limit. I needed more sleep and adjusted by sending many of my lieutenants on evening activities with the idea that it was great development for them, and it was. As before, I had to be so careful about how I positioned myself at meetings or in elevators. In general, I tried to stay at a distance from others, because

I didn't want them looking me in the face too closely. On days when I needed the privacy of my office, I used the phone to handle what I normally would have taken care of in person.

I learned how to compensate, how to situate myself, what kind of distance to keep between me and other people—and it worked. I would not have persisted in my pretense if it had affected my ability to perform. As it was, I continued to achieve all the goals designated for me. My team was the top performing team in the nation, and I had first-rate people working with me. I will repeat that the circumstances of my particular position allowed me to do this. Certainly, it would be very difficult for most people to maneuver in this way.

After five or six treatments, my fingernails and toenails turned black. I've always had regular manicures anyway, and my nail polish easily hid the discoloration. I told my manicurist a diet problem was causing it. Then, slowly but surely, over a period of a few weeks, the nails started falling off. When the first one went, I put a band-aid over the nail bed, and said I slammed my finger in the car door. When the second one bit the dust, I said I had dropped a flowerpot on it. I used the same excuse for the third one, even though I never planted flowers. Eventually, the escalating rate of nail loss required a systemic excuse, prompting me to tell my manicurist that my blood pressure medication was causing it—although I don't take medication for blood pressure. (Later she developed hypertension and refused to take medication for fear of losing her fingernails. The poor woman risked hospitalization before she finally consented to treatment!)

Ironically—or maybe not so ironically—at work, I had the best year ever from a performance standpoint. I earned the largest incentive payment I personally had ever received. I was promoted again and took on more responsibility. The person I reported to was in San Francisco, and I saw that individual very rarely, maybe a few times a year.

Not being truthful bothered me, though. As I have mentioned, I grew up with a deep respect for morality and truthfulness and could never have survived twenty years dealing with a life-threatening disease without a keen spiritual strength. I had learned to spin tales and make up excuses so well that it disturbed me, but all the deception derived from my dedication to get rid of this cancer and go back to a normal life. The CAT scans kept showing the tumor in my liver—so I kept taking the chemo, masking its side effects, and guarding that whole portion of my life.

> *The cost of a thing is the amount of what I call life which is required to be exchanged for it, immediately or in the long run.*
>
> ~Henry David Thoreau

My angel corps, the small group of friends who had sustained me for so long, kept right on caring for me. They gave me my meals and took me to the doctor and to my chemotherapy treatments. They listened when I needed to talk, and they encouraged me continuously. I am grateful for every meal they fed me, every errand they ran, and every time they soothed my discomfort. They are dearer to me than any treasure; they are my most trusted and dependable companions.

In spite of all my determination, as the treatments continued, I was fading. Imaging studies showed little change in the tumor in the liver. I insisted on more and more chemotherapy to shrink it. The doctor wanted to space the doses further apart, to give my body time to recover, but I was intent on getting my cancer back into remission. Fighting the fight consumed me. I relied on medications to treat all my side effects, including the mild nausea I eventually experienced.

I remember one Sunday afternoon I just sat on the sofa crying, with a blanket over my head. I couldn't even eat soft scrambled eggs due to the ulcers in my mouth. I didn't know how much longer I could push myself. Crying was a rare event for me, and my friends never saw me in the condition I was in that day. Johnlyn witnessed my despair. She asked to go with me to my upcoming visit to the doctor when another chemo treatment was scheduled.

The day of the appointment arrived. My doctor, whom I love and respect so much, walked into the room and looked at me. I believe she knew I was wearing out. She had been growing more and more concerned that we were reaching the point at which the treatment was worse than the disease—but the last thing I ever wanted to hear her say was that I couldn't have more chemotherapy because it was causing too many side effects.

Taking a seat beside me, my doctor said, "You look tired. On a scale of one to ten, with ten being the most fatigue, and zero being the least fatigue, what is your fatigue level?"

"Oh, a three." I said.

At that point, Johnlyn did what I suppose angels do. She said, "Kay, I've never interrupted you because these visits are between you and your doctor, but I'm afraid I have to intercede here. I think you're not being quite straight with the doctor."

My doctor smiled kindly at me and asked again, "From one to ten, what would you say your fatigue level would be?"

I tried again. "Well, maybe I'm a five."

Johnlyn spoke up once more. "Don't you really think you're an eight or a nine on a good day?"

The time had come. I had to face my condition. "Yes, actually I guess I am about an eight or a nine on a very good day."

"That's what I thought," my doctor said. "We need to stop the chemo because there's a fine line between treatment and doing real damage, and I think we're about to cross that line."

I knew the cancer was inside my liver, and it was large, maybe two and a half inches. I had to get rid of it. I said, "Well, what can we do? I still have a tumor showing up on the CAT scan. Can't you just cut it out? When my cancer was treated with surgery in 1984, I went nearly twelve years without a recurrence." She explained that surgery wasn't the protocol for metastatic breast cancer.

"I don't care about protocol; I care about getting rid of this tumor," I said.

My doctor wanted to think about it and talk to a hepatic surgeon and also to consult her connections at M.D. Anderson and Mayo. She promised to get back in touch with me in a day or two.

This was it. I teetered on the brink in so many senses of the phrase. Tomorrow could bring news that would either quench my last hope . . . or ignite it in a bright new blaze.

7:

EXPOSING THE POSSIBLE

Not to assume it's impossible because you find it hard. But to recognize that if it's humanly possible, you can do it, too.

~Marcus Aurelius

I went back to work after my last scheduled chemotherapy—the one that never happened—calling on clients and generally taking care of what needed to be done, anxiously awaiting the call from my oncologist. I remember exactly when it came, at six o'clock in the evening as I was walking through the parking lot back to my office. My cell phone rang. The doctor said, "I want you to see this hepatic surgeon; he has at least agreed to meet you and review your case." The words delighted me. She had set up an appointment.

A few days passed, and I went to meet the hepatic surgeon. He is an extraordinary man, the head of surgery at a very large hospital in

Dallas. He had taught at Southwestern Medical School, and is renowned in his field.

"We do not do surgery on metastatic breast cancer," he told me. "That's not treatment protocol for stage four cancer."

"What am I going to do?" I asked. "I can't take anymore chemotherapy, so the only answer is to cut out the cancer that's still there."

"That's just not what's recommended," he told me again.

I would not—could not—let it go at that. "Doctor, I don't care what's recommended. Why can't you do this?"

At length, he consented at least to talking it over with my oncologist again, and he also wanted to have my case evaluated by a medical review board. My oncologist went to bat for me. She told the hepatic surgeon that I was indeed a candidate for the type of surgery I desired. "She has long periods of remission," she told him. "Her cancer is obviously not an aggressive type of malignancy; she's lived with it eighteen years at this point. Her DNA naturally fights it and puts it into these long periods of remission. She's young. She's healthy. She takes good care of herself. She's got a good attitude. I think we owe it to her to explore this option."

The surgeon wasn't immediately sold on the idea. Eventually I found out that he had performed this kind of surgery perhaps twice before. Both of the former patients were women with breast cancer metastatic to the liver and both were alive a couple of years after the surgery. It was still very much an experimental procedure, certainly not for everyone with liver metastases, and the surgeon had to choose his patients carefully.

He went to his review board and discussed it. Within a couple of weeks, I received a call from him on my cell phone. He told me, "I've decided to take a chance on you." I was absolutely thrilled. I felt the hand of God on my shoulder. Now I had a fighting chance. I was a candidate for surgery after all, with the opportunity to have this malignancy cut out of my body.

The surgeon wanted me to have extensive tests in order to be sure there was no cancer anywhere except my liver. I underwent the tests, and again I felt the presence of God with me. There was no indication of cancer in my brain, in my lungs, in my pancreas, in my gall bladder, or in my bones—only this one lone nodule in the right lobe of my liver.

Unless you have believed, you will not understand.

~Isaiah 7:9

Both of the doctors cautioned me. A hepatic resection is major, major surgery. They counseled me on the risks, such as serious bleeding, since the liver is a very vascular organ. In addition, I was starting off in a weakened condition after six months of chemotherapy. I have abundant reserves, though, and every fiber of my being wanted to have this surgery. It was the only choice for me. I didn't accept the option of doing nothing more. My oncologist has recently said that she believes one of the reasons I have been successful in my treatments is that I have an internal radar which locks in on the pioneering options, the solutions that work for me. I am grateful that both she and my surgeon have a pioneering spirit as well!

Having a serious procedure of this sort, under cover, required some creative thinking on my part. I asked myself, "What kind of surgery can you have that knocks you out of work for six to eight weeks, but which people won't ask very many questions about?" I mulled it over and came up with a "woman thing." Surgery of that nature will cause most men to blush, look the other way, and forego the follow-up questions. That was it. I had my answer. I would simply say I was taking about six weeks of medical leave for surgery—I was going to have a hysterectomy. It was humorous to think of spreading that word because, of course, I had already had a hysterectomy back in 1986, at the time of the first fire drill. All of the people who knew about that, though, were long gone, and nobody would suspect a thing.

My mind was going a hundred miles an hour, scheming and planning. How could I carry out this subterfuge? I could say I didn't want any visitors in the hospital while having my hysterectomy, but I knew there would be well-wishers who'd still pop by and leave a flower. I absolutely could not have that. I wouldn't have Sybil on in the hospital—even I had to draw the line somewhere. I had no hair, and an unannounced visitor would bring me right out of the closet!

I came to the conclusion that I wouldn't tell anyone about the "hysterectomy" in advance. I would just say I was going on vacation, and then about two weeks into the "vacation," after I was already home from the hepatic surgery, I would contact the bank. I would say that it had become apparent I needed a hysterectomy, and that I didn't want any visitors in the hospital. I would be having it in the next few days and would be out for six weeks. My team of direct reports would run the business for me while I was out; I would be in contact by telephone if needed. I had my bases covered that way. No one could drop by the hospital and see me, because I would already be home by the time I told them I was going in. I could pull it off once again.

The day of the surgery was quite a day. I was so excited and so pumped up that nothing seemed quite real. Both doctors had tried hard to prepare me for what a major event it would be, but I never imagined how serious it was until after it happened. The surgeon came into the room where I was waiting and said the surgical team would administer the anesthesia, then while I was out, they would do one more scan to be sure that as of that moment, before they ever made an incision, I had no cancer anywhere else in my body. He told me that if they found cancer elsewhere, he would not do the surgery. I agreed, because of course, they couldn't. After that, the anesthesia overtook me.

The next five days were a fog. I have very few recollections of those days in the intensive care unit. The surgery had been long and messy. I had lost a lot of blood and required transfusions over the course of the next few days. I recollect hearing the doctor say, "She's not going to make it; we shouldn't have attempted this." I thought I was dying. I remember opening one eye and thinking, "I always thought it would be more special than this. I thought I would hear music and see angels, and maybe my mother and father would be there to greet me as I made the passage." Where were the angels? Why wasn't there a chorus or music, a trumpet sounding, a bright light?

When I finally began to come back to my senses, and was aware of my oncologist's visit, I asked if I was dying.

"No, why do you think that?" she asked.

"I thought I heard the doctor say that."

"No, the surgery was a success. The cancer is gone and you're going to recover."

Suddenly, I felt much better.

Eventually, they moved me to a private room. I was still extremely ill, though, and in a lot of pain. I had an incision twelve to fourteen inches long across my abdomen, and I couldn't sit up, let alone stand or walk. I couldn't even get my legs onto an ottoman without someone lifting them. Worse, I was miserably swollen. I had gained about forty pounds of fluid weight from all the IV solutions, and the pressure made it difficult to breathe. I couldn't imagine that my life would ever be normal after this.

Over the next few days, I was depressed, and I wondered if I had made the right decision in having such extreme surgery. I could see visitors—my brother, my sister-in-law, my niece, my nephew, and the very dear friends who knew about my surgery—but I had no energy. One morning my oncologist came into the room and leaned over me with a serious expression.

"Kay, I have to ask you a very important question," she said.

"What is that?" I asked, immediately more alert.

"Clinically speaking, is the second hysterectomy more painful than the first?" She didn't even crack a smile.

"You know what? It's a lot bigger deal than the first hysterectomy," I answered. We enjoyed a good laugh over it. She was always amused by the stories I fabricated to cover my medical dealings. She still mentions my second hysterectomy every once in a while and laughs.

My hospital stay grew tiresome and I longed to go home to sit in my comfortable chairs, surrounded by my own things. I knew my loving angel friends would care for me. Finally, after ten days, I was able to leave, and my friends came to help me. We soon discovered that my clothes didn't fit. I had worn a jogging suit on admission to the hospital, but with that extra forty pounds, it was a job to get me into it. Fortunately, it stretched enough to wear home, and my friends stuffed me into the car. When we reached home, I asked Toni to go to the store and buy the largest thing she could find for a nightshirt. She returned with a giant garment with a tag that said, "One size fits most." We shared a belly laugh over that one. I think laughter is a necessary part of healing. I've always been able to maintain a sense of humor and see the lighter side of life. There is humor in almost everything, if you look for it.

When I began my recovery at home, I couldn't walk ten steps without fatiguing. The fluid around my lungs prevented me from taking easy breaths, and even affected my speech. It also squeezed my stomach, suppressing my appetite. I was further down than I had ever been in my life. I knew I had only about six weeks to get back on my feet. We had to get started on the long road of rehabilitation immediately.

Toni stayed with me for a month, and she proved to be not only an angel, but also a coach. As a matter of fact, she actually wore a cap inscribed with the word "Coach," and she hung a whistle around her neck. Every morning, she weighed me. I was taking a diuretic and drinking twenty or thirty glasses of liquid a day in order to flush out the fluid I had accumulated.

I wanted to go outside, but my feet were too swollen for shoes. Thus confined to the indoors, I started walking in circles from one end of the house to the other. Toni counted the laps. At first, my progress was so painfully slow that it took fifteen minutes to make one lap, and I only had enough strength for one or two circuits. Soon, I was able to manage three or four, and eventually a dozen. Although I could see progress, the prolonged and tedious nature of it was disheartening. I went through horrible self-doubt, and wondered time and again if I'd ever be normal again. I remember once saying to Toni as I trudged around the circuit, "Isn't it amazing that life has come to this? The highlight of my day is being able to walk from one end of my house to the other—me, the woman who rides a bike a hundred miles a day." Very slowly, though, with daily effort, I shed the fluid, pound by pound. By the time I could make fifty and then seventy-five laps, I had lost fifteen pounds, and I could fill my lungs and move better.

My angel corps always made certain I had food, and I have to laugh when I remember the assortment of meals they provided after my appetite returned. Julie, a gourmet cook, often brought me healthy meals, but the only thing Toni could make was breakfast. She would consistently serve up a juicy plate of bacon and eggs—dietary fats notwithstanding. Johnlyn, the takeout queen, furnished many creative meals from different restaurants, but her forays into the kitchen never produced anything other than French toast or tacos. If another friend called when they knew Johnlyn was there, they'd often ask, "How are your tacos?" Although I meticulously choose healthy foods under normal circumstances, I don't remember ever turning down the bacon or the tacos!

Eventually it occurred to me that in the past, I didn't get fit all at once and, I certainly wasn't going to do so this time. It was a gradual process, and I had to have faith in it. I knew I could rehabilitate myself in time. The doctors had given me all kinds of exercises to do; I just had to persist.

Meanwhile, I made frequent visits to the doctor and had various tests to determine how my liver was recovering. They would do CAT scans, and I would look at the images with the hepatic surgeon, watching the progress as my liver regenerated. The liver can regrow, just as a lizard's lost tail can. They had removed the right lobe of my liver, and now the left lobe was growing to fill the void. The regenerated liver doesn't form distinct lobes as it once had, but grows as a single segment, in a somewhat spherical shape. After two or three months, I had a liver that was over eighty-five percent of its original size, and most importantly, it was perfectly healthy with no cancer anywhere.

As I got closer to returning to work, I remember sitting outside, having coffee by the pool one day in May, thinking about something I had once read. The article had said that there are only two ways to live life: one way is

The soul becomes dyed with the color of its thoughts.

~Marcus Aurelius

as though nothing is a miracle, and the other is as though everything is a miracle. You have to be like Peter Pan, finding Neverland. You have to believe in yourself, in others, and in a higher power. Then you have to just give it over. I expected a miracle. I prayed for a miracle, and I believe I received one, because I have the gift of good health back. I have the gift of each and every new day, and the opportunity to make the most of those days. I think time and time again, that true happiness is a quality of thought. It's a state of mind. It's a way of being. It's a choice.

8:

BE IT LIFE OR DEATH

Be it life or death, we crave only reality. If we are really dying, let us hear the rattle in our throats and feel cold in the extremities; if we are alive, let us go about our business.

~Henry David Thoreau

In recent years, I reread *Walden*, by Henry David Thoreau, and discovered words that captured my mindset after rehabilitation from serious surgery and the chemotherapy that preceded it. By returning to work, I was going about my business in a literal, as well as a figurative, sense. I leapt into it, feeling very much alive and very grateful to God that I had my life back. I invested my spirit and my enthusiasm into a profession I loved—one that had motivated and rewarded me well.

At fifty-seven years old, I was the old Kay again, ready to go—or so I thought at the time. Although there was something different about me when I returned to work this last time, it wasn't the change in myself that I first noticed.

What immediately came to my attention was that my company was not its old self, the entity I had spent most of my adult life with, growing and developing. Over the years, my financial institution kept getting larger and larger. It was now one of the largest in the world, a very different business from the one I had joined in the mid 1970s. It was interesting and exciting to sit back and take stock of how the industry had changed during the course of my career.

There was a flip side to the evolution of the institution, though—and it was stressful. A tremendous amount of internal change was brewing. Two huge segments of the company were merging—and they were segments of such magnitude that they had the impact of whole companies merging. As in the past, these maneuverings created tremendous anxiety and uncertainty. Soon the restructuring, the refocusing, and the layoffs consumed me.

On top of all the other changes, a great deal of political upheaval was occurring.

Times of corporate positioning always strain business relationships—even long-standing and close ones. The concerns people feel for their future security cause them to push others away, to scramble for their own place in the hierarchy. I'd never enjoyed that part of corporate America, nor had I been a smooth politician. I prided myself on calling a spade a spade. I applied my sense of justice and ethics, and I didn't always say what was politically correct.

Endless committees tied up my days and most of my nights. We needed to get a fix on what this restructuring would look like, what qualities suitable teammates would have, who and what would fit into the new organization, and what we would keep, what we would outsource, and what we would shut down. There was no time to dwell on my past medical experiences or on much of anything except what was going on in my immediate work environment.

After a few months of the most chaotic reorganization I had yet experienced, I realized that something had changed within me, had altered my perspective. Much of what was happening around me now seemed trivial or frivolous, undeserving of my rapt attention. Something tugged at me mentally and emotionally, demanding that I redirect my intensity and my efforts to more meaningful pursuits. My foundation of spirituality, always a wellspring for me, was now coming to the forefront.

Then, one day as I sat in my office, surrounded by glass, high in a skyscraper in downtown Dallas, the idea of retirement suddenly came to me. It may sound odd that I had never thought particularly about the end of my career or life after

Whatever prepares you for death enhances life.

~Stephen Levine

work, but that's the truth. I knew that someday I would have to retire, but going back to work had always been my saving grace. My profession put structure around me and gave me a purpose. I was a bank executive; that's how I defined myself. I believe work seduced me, just as a drink seduces an alcoholic. I kept being tempted by one more year, by one more achievement, by one more professional accomplishment.

I had thought of the possibility of not working, of course, when a cancer crisis forced me to, but when I returned to work, I would always bypass those thoughts again. This time, though, my mind wandered, searching for something else. Now what beckoned to me was not another year as a banker, not another new team to lead, not another department to oversee. It was something less defined, but nonetheless compelling, like the anticipation of fine wine or a journey yet to be taken.

Sitting in my office that day, viewing the Dallas skyline, I realized that I wanted and needed to let go of work. Maybe I would even shed Sybil. I wanted to become who I really was: a cancer survivor. I remember shaking my head and wondering what was happening to me. My thoughts were entering uncharted territory. I allowed myself to think beyond life as a banker. It was a bit frightening to imagine what I would do if not banking. It was all I had ever done— that is, all I had ever done besides dealing with cancer—for the last twenty years.

Once I began to think in terms of doing something different, I knew what I wanted was to give back in some way, to be able to help others struggling with cancer, or some other type of life-altering crisis. Close upon the heels of that revelation came a second revelation: it was impossible for me to help others while I was in the closet with my cancer, and I wasn't going to come out of the closet at work. It was clear, then, that I would have to leave.

It just seemed like the right time. I had proven to myself that I could get through what was now stage four cancer. I'd not only survived the cancer and its difficult treatment, but once again, I'd done it in secret, while succeeding at my profession. I had been back for about a year at this time, and thus I had also satisfied whatever force continually drove me to get back to work. To quote Ecclesiastes, "For everything there is a season, and a time for every matter under heaven." The season was changing for me. It was time to move on.

Within about a week, I made the decision to retire. I had thirty years with the company, and because of my age, almost fifty-eight, and my length of service, I would be able to take full retirement. Once I made that decision, as with almost everything else in my life, I didn't look back. I had done a lot of succession planning, and capable team members were ready to step up. I made the announcement that I was going to retire, and I believe it surprised a lot of people.

They threw a grand party in my honor, held at an elegant Dallas hotel. The number of people in attendance bowled me over. People from all over the world—literally—were there. Wonderful work family and acquaintances, scores of them, made my heart glow with their presence. Some of the work relationships went back thirty years, and included many people who had gone to other companies. Of course my brother, my sister-in-law, and my nephew came, and also my angel corps. It was a wonderful send-off, and all of it thrilled me—the toasting and roasting, the delightful reminiscing, the speeches, and the marvelous good humor. The drinks flowed freely, the food was superb, and the music was fabulous.

When it was time for me to say my farewells, emotion almost overwhelmed me, but then an inner strength took over. Someone handed me a microphone, and I thanked people for coming and said all the expected things. Then I said, "I want to talk a minute about my future plans. One of the things I'd really like to do is to write a book." I knew that as I uttered the words, those around me imagined I was anticipating writing a book about banking or leadership, how to motivate people, how to raise the bar, or how to achieve professionally. But I continued, "The book I want to write is about surviving cancer." I saw jaws drop, flabbergasted expressions. I continued. "I have been dealing with cancer for twenty of my thirty years in banking with this company. I have chosen to do it privately, and now I want to openly acknowledge and talk about my cancer."

I can not describe the incredible sense of freedom I felt in that moment. Now I could look people in the eye and speak frankly about my cancer. I could race for the cure, holding the banner high, wearing proudly the mantle of survivor. I never knew how much stress I was under, trying to keep Sybil a secret, until I could finally reveal myself. I felt more complete, more accepting, more real. My cancer was "me," just as much as was my face or my work ethic or my love of classical music. Now I could express it openly. At last, I was out of the closet with cancer.

9:

BRANDED BY OPINIONS

We are not troubled by things, but by the
opinions which we have of things.

~Epictetus

Now that you know my story, I want to delve deeper into my reasons for concealing my cancer and my treatment. I stayed in the corporate closet with cancer because I did not want to be branded by opinions. Did I fear my company's policies? No. Being in the upper echelons of management, I know for a fact there was no danger of open discrimination against those with health problems. Strictly speaking, no risk of being fired for having cancer existed. Yet I did fear losing my job. Why? Because an insidious peril lurked within the workplace, and for that matter, outside it, too. I am speaking of the kind of judgment cast upon those with cancer—judgment by individuals who may happen to be co-workers, neighbors, friends, strangers, or employers.

Perhaps, by writing this book, I can call attention to the subtle, yet pervasive prejudice we all have against those perceived as "flawed." Diseases and handicaps of all kinds carry a stigma beyond any actual weakness that the disease may cause. This bias is so deeply ingrained in us that we are mostly unaware of it. Our disregard of those with health disorders is often—perhaps even usually—unspoken.

I derive evidence for this observation from the many interactions I have had, both with people who did not know of my cancer and those who did. A recent conversation with a human resources manager from a Fortune 500 company reinforced my ideas on the subject. She remarked that in spite of current laws that offer significant protection for employees, the reaction of individual managers cannot be guaranteed. She stated further that a particular decision-maker "might not include [someone with cancer] in business opportunities that would result in her continued success and growth." Most importantly, she believes that such an exclusion can easily be based not on prognosis, but on negative assumptions regarding an employee's ability to recover, to perform fully, to remain focused, and she adds that "the decision-makers unfortunately often have those stereotypical kinds of feelings."

Taking my exploration of the silent dismissive attitude toward illness a step further, I believe that the assumptions alluded to above are often unknown to us, even when they come from within! For this assertion, I derive evidence from my own covert thoughts about my disease. Although I honestly and openly proclaim myself to be of sound health, not spent or lessened by cancer, not marred by it in any way, I recently caught myself saying the words, "I'm a perfectionist. Sick people are not perfect, and I could not be less than perfect."

If I myself saw cancer as making me imperfect as a person, how could I expect others to see me as unimpaired? For twenty of my thirty career years, I was fighting for survival from an all-consuming disease and at the same time fighting almost daily for a chair at the executive table . . . merger, after merger, after merger. The fierceness of the competition eventually plucked out not only those with observable deficiencies in performance, or drive, or talent. It also ousted those with far less objectionable shortcomings.

"Top grading" describes our method for selecting the best of the best. Once associates with obvious insufficiencies were weeded out, that left a group of good performers. When it was time for the next round of layoffs, one of those good performers had to go, and of course, the one with a slightly less desirable performance was dropped. When circumstances required yet more cuts, a group of very good performers had to be culled, and the player with only a shade less desirable qualities was discharged. Thus, after a series of reductions, the associates left in place were all excellent, top performers. Even the faintest hint of "weakness" spelled doom, since invariably there would be yet another round of downsizing, and someone else would have to leave.

Stewing inside a corporate culture of this nature, I was constantly on guard. If I let my cancer and my ongoing treatments be known, how could I ever be sure that somewhere along the line I wouldn't be the victim of someone's undercurrent thoughts? "Kay is performing well enough, but she doesn't seem as energetic as she used to be." "Kay's leadership is top-notch, but how much longer can she keep it up, with all her outside distractions?" I'm not saying my colleagues would ever have given voice to these thoughts, even behind closed doors. I don't think that the many fine people I worked with would have intentionally given me short shrift, or would necessarily even have been conscious of their thought processes. I do believe, though, that in the environment of top grading, it wouldn't have taken too many mergers for others in decision-making positions to edge me out.

And I faced this dilemma on two fronts. What if the people under me had known of my cancer? I was able to generate prime production because I led prime associates. I led an A-team because I commanded the respect and the loyalty to pull grade-A work out of my team members. If they knew about my cancer, they may well have doubted my future and looked for security elsewhere. And even if they stayed with me, who's to say that my team could have achieved the same performance levels if they perceived me as diminished, scarred, somehow not quite up to the task of leading?

There are understandable reasons for our attitude toward sickness. A major one is undoubtedly that any malady in others mirrors our own vulnerability. It is discomforting to come face to face with serious conditions, whether cancer, lameness, blindness, or other disorders. We normally carry with us a healthy denial that dreadful things can happen to us, and we don't like reminders to the contrary. Thus, it may be emotionally easier to dissociate from a person with cancer than to interact with him or her.

We can also feel fear of another's illness. This may stem from a natural desire to avoid communicable disease, perhaps dating back to less enlightened eras when people did not know which conditions could be transmitted from person to person. Perhaps in even the most educated among us, there remains a trace of superstition that we can "catch" cancer.

Other age-old notions may cling to our psyches, also. Primitive societies probably could not afford affliction in their midst. With marginal resources and constant outside dangers, members with even temporary impediments may have exposed the group to increased risk.

Even if we feel no reluctance to interact with individuals who have a disease, our mindset may still cause us to react in a deleterious way. Sympathy, although offered with the best intentions, can be a curse to those who receive it. A hairsbreadth separates caring from condescending. When I was undergoing treatment, sympathy from others made me feel sick.

Cloaked discrimination, whether from a reluctance to face our own fears, or from a desire to coddle, can undermine the will and the confidence of a cancer patient. It can make those with a serious disease see themselves as unfit, as incompetent, or as incapable, and thus become a self-fulfilling prophecy. If we become aware of our own hidden prejudices against those with conditions that are not society's ideal, we can boost those individuals far more than any amount of sympathy ever would.

*Search not a wound
too deep lest thou
make a new one.*

~Thomas Fuller, MD

My thesaurus demonstrates exactly how we tend to think of disease. Synonyms for "disease" include blight, contamination, debility, decrepitude, feebleness, infirmity, sickliness, and unsoundness. Synonyms for "sick" include declining, defective, frail, impaired, imperfect, rickety, rotten, and wobbly!

Of course, there are certainly many stages of disease and many conditions that cause actual impairment. I don't deny that there were times in the course of my treatment when I was physically weakened, and even mentally overwhelmed. I am not implying that "infirmity" is never a part of disease. But I am drawing a line—a big, bold line—between the weakness a condition may cause in REALITY and the weakness that is PERCEIVED in the minds of onlookers.

When I received a promotion during a course of chemotherapy, and in the midst of unremitting and intense competition, I proved that my cancer did not make me weak in the sense of leadership, decision-making, analyzing, strategizing, or any other aspect of job performance. I hope that in making this point, I can punch a hole in preconceived notions of what cancer—or other serious disease—affects. I hope I can make you pause and reconsider what you may expect of a cancer "victim." I hope I can make you reflect on the resilience of human nature, on the strength of the human will, and on the power of the human mind. I hope I can release from you any sense of hopelessness in the face of a serious condition, either your own or someone else's.

Epilogue:

Ask Not Good Fortune

Afoot and lighthearted, I take to the open road,
Healthy, free, the world before me
The long brown path before me
leading wherever I choose.
Henceforth, I ask not good fortune,
I myself am good fortune,
Henceforth I whimper no more,
postpone no more, need nothing
Done with indoor complaints,
libraries, querulous criticisms,
Strong and content
I travel the open road.

~Walt Whitman

Volumes and volumes of books have been written about and by cancer survivors, often by celebrities, politicians, or others in prominent positions. For that very reason, I almost didn't tell my story. I thought, "Who am I to write a book? Who would care? Who would read it?" But, through the gentle encouragement of my oncologist, I gained insight into the fact that my approach to coping with cancer was unusual. I really didn't know that. Many people go to work, continue to perform, or manage family life while coping with this disease. My situation simply didn't seem any different. I believe I had gotten so good at playing the game that I had forgotten that it may have been extraordinary.

I'm writing this book as my gift. It's my passion now and my purpose. I don't know for certain why I've been given this opportunity, but I believe it is to help other cancer survivors. I hope my ideas about the subtle prejudice those with serious health conditions face can help all of us take a look at our own attitudes. I believe we can improve our reactions and responses if we examine what colors our perceptions. Most of all, I hope I can be an inspiration to someone, even just one person, who is lost in the darkness of the disease. Perhaps my story can help someone with cancer see that a place that appears to be the end, in reality might be the beginning.

There is a constant ebb and flow to one's life. A person is born all at once, but she or he does not live all at once. Life is a process, not an event. Likewise, the meaning of an individual life is ongoing, evolving. Our paths may turn unexpected corners, but as long as we still breathe, we can make choices that influence the new direction for better or for worse. As our situation changes, new purposes unfold, and new ways to achieve fulfillment present themselves. Desiderius Erasmus, Dutch author, philosopher, and scholar of the sixteenth century, tells us, "Give light, and the darkness will disappear of itself."

I believe that the time has come to shine a light on the darkness of cancer. Every individual should understand that the diagnosis of many malignancies no longer constitutes a death sentence. To quote a section from the Web site for the American Cancer Society (www. cancer.org):

> *The risk of being diagnosed with cancer and the risk of dying of cancer have decreased since the early 1990s. Fewer than half the people diagnosed with cancer today will die of the disease. Some are completely cured, and many more people survive for years with*

*a good quality of life, thanks to treatments
that control many types of cancer.*

And from the Web site maintained by the National Cancer Institute (Cancer Progress Report - 2003 Update, National Cancer Institute, NIH, DHHS, Bethesda, MD, February 2004, http://progressreport.cancer.gov/):

*More and more people are benefiting
from the early detection of cancer and its
successful treatment. These medical advances
are improving both quality of life and length
of survival, permitting many survivors to
continue full and productive lives at home
and at work.*

We'll never know how many people keep their cancer hidden in the closet. We'll never know how many people celebrate quiet victories over cancer or other diseases. I suspect that there are many others who have kept serious health problems a secret, who feared, as I did, the consequences of revelation. If we knew how many people have successfully hidden cancer experiences and continued on in the workplace with satisfactory performance, we may be surprised. Perhaps myths about the inevitable devastation of cancer could be put to rest.

A number of years ago, my oncologist—dear friend and physician that she is—urged me to retire to help relieve my stress. I refused, contending that the stress was what fueled me! Now I find that something altogether different fuels me: the exquisite concept of being and not doing. It involves enriching life by exalting the moment. When you accept cancer, I think you really begin to live. Not necessarily to do, but to live, to appreciate how extraordinary simple moments can be. When you focus on being and not doing, you experience the paradox of finding an infinite amount of time in the finite moment you have.

My oncologist sum- *The butterfly counts not* med up my attitude pre- *months but moments,* cisely when she recalled *and has time enough.* an announcement I made

~Rabindranath Tagore

to her after I recovered from my liver surgery: "I just bought a Jaguar, and it wasn't the small one." I remember calling her office while I was considering retiring, and asking how long I could reasonably expect to live, as I needed "a number" for my financial advisor to plug into our calculations! Judging from what my oncologist has since said, I think I impressed her by stating bluntly that I intended to spend all my money. She understood that I wasn't spending my money because I was dying, but because I was living.

"Healthy, free, the world before me," I find the "path before me leading wherever I choose." I spent my first year of retirement traveling around the world. The Mediterranean dazzled me from the awe-inspiring cathedrals of France to the exotic architecture of Turkey. Archeological excavation in Greece delighted me, and the possibility of the lost city of Atlantis off the coast of Santorini intrigued me. I experienced the luxury of a trans-Atlantic crossing on the Queen Mary II during her inaugural year, the regal mysteries of Russia, and the pristine and remote allure of Scandinavia. An Alaskan train trip to Mount McKinley and a balloon excursion over the red rock canyons of Sedona, Arizona, charmed me. From snowshoeing and dog-sledding in Canada to the lush vistas of Hawaii, I celebrated my life and my health.

My passions have always included playing golf, enjoying classical music, and educating myself about vineyards and wine production. Having the time to indulge myself with these pastimes gratifies me, and at the same time, it whets my appetite for yet more areas of exploration. Cooking and photography classes tempt me in the coming year.

In my second year of retirement, writing this book has been my fuel and my passion, each page laced with my prayers. Perhaps I can cast enough light to make the darkness disappear for someone, somewhere, who is in the closet with cancer.

There's not much more to say in this book, but there's a lot more for me to do in this world. I pray daily that my journey is a long one, but if it is cut short for any reason, I feel that I have accomplished what was my calling. My life has been, and continues to be, very open and very positive and very happy. And for that, I am most thankful.

THE END